Wildfire, Candleflame

Wildfire, Candleflame

To Slahania —
all best wishes,

by

David D. Horowitz

David D. Horowitz

Rose Alley Press
Seattle, Washington

Published in the United States of America by Rose Alley Press

For information, please contact the publisher:

Rose Alley Press
David D. Horowitz, President
4203 Brooklyn Avenue NE, #103A
Seattle, WA 98105-5911
Telephone: 206-633-2725
E-mail: rosealleypress@juno.com
Web site: www.rosealleypress.com

The author gratefully acknowledges that the following poems in this book first appeared, or will appear, in the following publications:

Candelabrum: "Gift," "In Seeming Silence," "Other Galaxies," "Skyline Gull,"
    "To Integrity"
HA!: "Bird Person," "Bounce," "Libido," "Literary Fame," "Quotidian Victorious,"
    "To Some Sports Fans," "Tribes"
The Lyric: "Push and Pause"
Marble: "Ashcan Cathedral," "Negotiation"
Moon Upside Down, Stars in Rows: "Affix," "Rush Hour"
NW Ink: "Potluck"
Northwind Anthology 2004: "Loss"
The New Formalist: "Each Wing Alive," "For You to See," "Gull," "Power"
Splizz: "First," "Of a Young Woman Who Writes"
Tucumcari Literary Review: "Funny to a Few"
Tundra: "Pornography," "Of a Friend's Modeling," "Libido"

ISBN 0-9745024-3-X

Front-cover photograph: "The beach was as ghastly as nuclear winter."
Copyright © 2005 by Jason Wells. For more information about Jason Wells'
photography, visit www.crispyneurons.com.

Printed in the United States of America

ACKNOWLEDGEMENTS

I want to thank my mother, Ruth Horowitz, for her unstinting support; Victoria Ford, Michael Spence, and Michael Dylan Welch for suggesting improvements to the manuscript of this book; Sharon E. Svendsen, CEO of Writers' Haven Press, for offering me various wonderful opportunities; and J. Glenn Evans, Barbara Evans, Christopher J. Jarmick, and all the fine people who schedule and promote literary readings.

CONTENTS

Wildfire, Candleflame

Each Wing Alive

Gulls roost in downdraft float
   And updraft boomerang
   And coast, wheel, and hang
Above the harbor, circling over boat
And passersby. They loop
   Back through skyline, and glide
   Thermal, each wing alive
To wind's inflections, in swoop
And swoon. They seem to race
   Yet scamper and careen
   Above the day's routine
That craves unscheduled grace.

Rush Hour

Now headlights pour, recede to scarlet dots,
And streetlamps plink and glow awake
As twilight rediscovers clarity.

The refugees from downtown parking lots
Fill freeways curving past the hills and lake
To alternately zoom ahead and stall,

Bunch homeward, carmine echo coating freeway wall.
In sky, magenta shadow fringes cloud;
Below, the evergreens seem silhouettes.

Now, packed in with commuter crowd
Elated over leisure, worried over debts,
Exhausted by new strains each working week,

Some riders fume; some fill with charity
And bless; and some can only sigh
And let their hearts suffuse with sky.

Note

You strain and strive to yield from phrase
And jotting: poetry. On sunny days
You often sit indoors to write,
Then stroll your neighborhood the lamplit night
With pen and pad in pocket, scrawled black ink
Preserving impulse. Thought and image link
On Post-It Note that might yet seed
A poem many millions read.

Potluck

*—for the 2003 Holiday Dinner of
the Pacific NW Writers Association*

Adhesive name tags helped us grin and greet
Near tables laden—chilled white wine
And apple cider, marinated meat
And pasta salad, cherry pie
And chocolate cake. We nibbled, once in line,

On conversation's appetizers: *When
Did you join? What do you write? Did
You serve yet on our board?* And then
We sat, ate, learned. "What" turned to "why,"
And questions, voices flowered. No one hid

Or boasted. Each could listen, each was heard;
Though different, each devours the written word.

First

Not domination nor submission
But balance, trade. Then, ambition
Might flower gold. Blend ability
With heroism of humility.
For rose to bloom the earth and rain must nourish,
And eloquence must listen first to flourish.

Of a Young Woman Who Writes

Words help her formulate opinions
And soothe the wounded friend,
Learn science, history, and blend
Perceptions into nascent wisdom.
But more—from her favorite poem
She learns words can be companions.

Faraway Within

The darkest night reveals the faintest stars
And depth throughout the heart—its violence
And vengeance for its wounds and scars
And its serenity and silence.
Tonight such darkness nestles sky: it hears
Each moment's longing, each lifetime's tears.

To an Excellent Mother

*—for Elizabeth
and Kelsey*

Sky in which to dream, ground on which to grow,
And self-esteem to dare and doubt and seek:
In your daughter's heart you plant the seed
Of courage, and in her mind the need to know.
Your love strengthens her. You want her kind, not meek;
Most buds, to blossom, must weather cold, wind, and snow.

Spectrum

More error, fakery, and glitch
Than excellence. More fluff and kitsch
Than treasure. More duplicity
And hype than authenticity.
You know, so often offered stems
Not flowers, huckstered paste not gems.
You seldom quit—but you returned
And deeper for each lapse. You learned
The rose of dusk, the eloquence
Of honesty in many tints.

Affix

Scotch Tape, your role is clear.
Stick with it. Persevere.
Seal up container lids; rejoin torn
Parts. Bridge the disparate
And calm the desperate,
And help the broken feel reborn.

To a Delightfully Balanced Young Woman

I

You're warm yet efficient
And self-sufficient
Yet kind. Am I deficient?
I cannot find
Fault with you.
You seem
A dream,
And yet you're earthy, too!

II

Your beauty, charm, and warmth could stoke, seduce
Desire; your mere grin could flutter blood;
Your gentlest touch or laugh could trigger flood
Of fantasy no reason could reduce.
May such a gift yield love for you, your bud
Bloom sweetest fruit, not seeds of bitter juice
From jealousy's abuse.

Verse Aid Kit

Above horizon, dusk's lagoon
Extends its shore, its opal seep
To silhouetted range, maroon-
Illuminated breadth of deep

Silence. Headlines blare more death
And bleeding. Traffic zips and zooms.
One human heart achieves new depth.
Hope whispers verse as terror looms.

WILDFIRE, CANDLEFLAME

It's Ours!

Holy sights
Breed hellish fights.

To an Islamic Extremist

You read and study, venerate each *sura*
And grow so wise you glow with righteous calm.
You think there's nothing now you aren't sure of—
Like that full school bus you're about to bomb.

Culture Shock

The bomb erased the flat's façade,
    Killed residents of every story.
The bombers celebrated God,
    This proof of His support and glory.

Lost

First piqued his raging bombast,
Then surged the suicide's bomb blast.
A smash with some; for most a tragic
Why—ten lives lost in morning traffic
For nothing. Ambulances clog an inter-
Section. There's a leg like a splinter
As blood mists headlines and window chips.
Hearts melt, and minds harden behind solemn lips.

Funny to a Few

We join the world of checkpoint, secret eye, and frisk,
Of paranoia minimizing risk.
Defending liberty, we choose to limit same.
Now pranksters needn't shoot, merely aim.

Fashion News

What's hot these days in recreation?
Fire-bombing and assassination.

Knowledge

We learn who so meticulously dupes
Our country's spies and killed so many troops.
The dead stay dead, though. None feel merry
On journeys to the cemetery
Or grin because they grieve in groups.

Quotidian Victorious

The hero thrusts his sword and conquers
But finds that ruling drives him bonkers.

Grief

Tolerance feels terribly sad:
Terrorism has become a fad.

Catharsis

Yes, speak strongly. Purge, expiate, vent!
Now, go understand—not just avenge.

Loss

Though I'm a Cubbies fan I will not castigate and blame.
Five soldiers lost their lives today. The Cubs just lost a game.

Fire, Ice, Whatever

A bomb might fall
    That none could stop or capture.
It might kill all
    And won't be like the rapture.

Spring Poem

Atomic weapons, talk of "nukes"
Redominate the nightly news,
And Armageddon seems to loom
As songbirds trill and daisies bloom.

Negotiation

Just several steps of understanding
Could yield enough for peace.
Climb the staircase: on a landing
Rest but do not cease.

Soldier, Iraq 2004

Your prayers back home might not deter more violence
But utter them, like candlelight in silence.

Just Back

I need to kiss and hug my wife and cherish
Reunion time. My armored tan Humvee
Becomes our little Chevy, and we'll drive
Around the city, grateful we're alive.
I need to sleep in my old bed, then wake
And visit friends and down a beer and steak
And celebrate this comeback victory.
I'm proud of how I served
Though still a bit unnerved:
How quickly we can perish.

Written in Time of War

War's inflammation sears and rends
Old half-healed wounds of left and right,
And feud can escalate to fight.
We disagree, yet tonight friends
Still, we're aware of the battlefield
Where bombs obliterate every shield.

Now, dispute could yield the snub,
And loyalties of petition
And march and one's position
On X and Y can serve a club
When verse and wit can yet precede
Such grouping. Tonight we banter, laugh, and read.

The Lamps

We might endure atomic war.
I offer you no blessing, prayer,
Or manifesto, promised door
To peace and comfort. I scare
As easily as most. Just now I stroll
This ruby-opal dusk through city park
And breathe treed calm and stroke
Leaves, flowers, needles, bark.
I undeadline, unstress. We might
Endure atomic war. A galaxy
Of lamps illuminates the dark tonight
As usual. This is prayer enough for me.

THOUGH NONE MIGHT WATCH

To Integrity

Let power press its nasty lever
To have you harassed night and day.
Stay
Honest forever.

In Context

Keep your integrity despite your pain—
That star outlasts this hurricane.

A Long Run

Enthusiasts shout, denounce, and chant!
You, though, prefer reflection challenging cant,
Striding integrity's marathon
Even when none look on.

❋   ❋   ❋

Muster

Despair can't lift a fork or spoon
Or rise from bed this afternoon.
Despair can't budge, and only breathes
Enough to live as sadness breeds
More minutes. Hours. Days. More slopes
Descending from forsaken hopes.
Tasks tower. Errands shadow. Life
Requires motion, water, light.
Decision might procrastinate,
And blood might yawn and circulate
A senseless route. Repair must stir
And busy, challenge self and spur
The disappointed heart. Now, work
To stand. Who knows where joy might lurk?

Headache Tablet

My heart stops clutching at my brain.
My blood enjoys some leisure,
Massages eyes, exhaling strain.
Now bloodflow is my leader.
What tightens scalp and clenches thought?
Ambition's seething, tasks and guilt,
Bills, shoulders full of should and ought.

I sigh, inhale, and stretch. Life's a gift.

For a Massage Practitioner

I

Each muscle breathes into the soul
Its natural smile now. You stroke and press
And ride a hand of lotion up a limb,
Releasing grit of worry, stress
Of deadline, strain of daily climb
To effort's summit, uncompleted goal.
Your fingers warm minutest tight
Stiff soreness I'd ignored for weeks and thaw
Away each knot each muscle, limb forgot.
Now pinch, poke, stroke, knead, squeeze, and paw
And soothe. You nurture every spot
Of stress. Each clench releases. Every bite
Of disappointment softens, salved. The soul
Remembers smile of a healthy whole.

II

You loosen stress's knots
And pressure's binding grip
At shoulder, neck, and hip
By stroking, thawing stiffened spots.

Like warm, warm water on
A too-tight lid hands sof-
ten muscle, tissue, suf-
fuse release into a dawn

Of relaxation, stiffness gone.

PAPER CLIPS

Monday, 6:30 a.m.

City sparkle penetrates blue dawn. A lake
Of lamps glitters below the office towers. A bus
Whooshes the other way, as luminous
Traffic streams downtown. The week is awake.

Stirring

Office kitchen, 8:00 a.m.
Workers stir coffee; it stirs them.

Of an Office Worker

You forage for meaning amidst routines
And scavenge for friendship amidst machines.

Repercussion

His boss's insult burned in his craw.
His own retort stayed locked in his jaw.

✻   ✻   ✻

Workday

Commuter headlights stream along the viaduct,
Most exiting towards office towers. Dawn
Mists Monday. Paycheck longings reconcile
Most to tension or tedium, feeling tucked
Into routine, though their hearts barely smile.
Who would grin, feeling like a peon or pawn?

Kids, deadlines, bills insist, yet friends console,
Vacations calm, and better supervisors
Appreciate the burdens, sensing whole
Selves behind sighs of their early risers.

Prosperity

Beneath dawn's saffron dune of mist, lamps blaze
And freeways speckle trickle. Crows cloud, gulls swoon
Across horizon, near the quarter moon
Above the silhouetted peak of snowy grays.

Commuters zoom to work, as quietude
And stillness yield, and deadlines hurry heart
To flurry into plan before tasks start.
Most sigh, and yet—they grumble gratitude,

Accepting as their toll for house and car
And children's college education
The daily slog at site or office, core
Of wealth, though eased by some vacation

And, often, weekends free. Now fewer lamps
Blaze. Traffic clogs the freeway ramps.

SILVER, SUNNY, GRAY

Dawn Scene

Horizon: auburn-aqua dawn
Illuminates the peaks
Below magenta cirrus streaks
Soon graying, wan.

So Sunny and Warm

The cloud that drifts above Ohio
Today, so sunny and warm,
As part of a storm
Doused Florida three days ago.

Gull

Feathered boomerang afloat above
Piers, skyline, traffic, boats, and bay,
Your overcast wings slant openings in gray
Breeze, hinting albatross and dove.

Skyline Gull

What a breeze
To skate the skyline, improvise
Flightpaths, then rise
And curl blue
Thermals down. What a view!

Free Flight

Spirit of a raptor
Resists a captor.

Intangible

Apricot glow fringes horizon's curtain.
It's sunny but raining. So little seems certain.

Dusk

Horizon past a silhouette of spire,
Branch, hilltop roofs, and wires
Screens opal-ruby fire.
Day focuses on data; I still require
A sky my heart admires.

Friends

Though friends betray, stars remain—
Sparkling tonight, after rain.

Furnished

Sky, after storms, clears. Stars burnish
Longing, yet constellate and furnish
Companionship, mitigating distance
With silent, silver persistence.

Teamwork

Sunlight can reveal
And shade soothe, not conceal.
Thus, candor can assert
While tact remains alert
To others feeling hurt
And charm, delight, and heal.

✼   ✼   ✼

Oatmeal

Like tofu, rice, or pasta, oatmeal's better
When blent—with raisins, apples, butter,
Brown sugar, cinnamon—and topped with cream.
Substantial breakfast with the sweetest steam,
It settles stomachs yet can fill and fuel
A morning's muscles. This tan, rough-edged gruel!

Honey

Sweet golden syrup
In little plastic bears and farmer-labeled jars,
You pollinate cups of tea
And harmonize candy bars.
You lace the morning toast, cheer up
Oatmeal, and top off hospitality

With nectar and balm.
More than rose, wine, or song, your purity
Can revive when blent.
Your sticky amber spooned in tea,
Or squeezed on toast, muffin, or bun,
Reminds the weary of sweetness, the blunt
Of subtlety.

Paper Towel

Let mama's jar of Roquefort dressing spill
On shelf in fridge or grit collect on sill
Or blinds or vent. I'll clean, absorb it all—
Dust bunnies by the floorboards in the hall
And chocolate syrup dribbled on the floor
And ketchup freckling up the basement door:
I'll clean it. White, I love getting dirty
Or saturated! This soldier does its duty:
You spray me, wipe a filthy countertop,
And leave it glowing. Now, much-used, please drop
Me into grave—a trash pail full of honest slop!

Partition Wall

Baby photos; pet snapshots, comic strips
Of common complaint;
Prayer of effort and restraint;
Saved birthday card; postcards from trips;
Company calendar, one week a spear
Of orange marker ink—vacation time near.

Countertop Communion

*—in praise of
co-worker bakers*

Beneath bulletin board of comic strips
And postcards from employees' trips,
Beside boxes of binder clips
A plate of home-baked cookies—chocolate chips! —

To retrieve for work station snack
So when you return to tack
And binder clip and paper stack
You sweeten brain and loosen back.

Meaning and Habit

An opal pool amongst the clouds and dark
   Horizon linger silence over peaks
   Beyond the highrise-cradled bay. Rose streaks
And cloud fringe glow beside a planet's spark.

Commuters crowd the freeway lanes, at last
   Pursuing private pleasures or more pay
   At second job. Bills due shape working day
Of most, the silent sky beyond so vast.

Secretarial Work

Stress sizzles through her silence, as she steeps
Some chamomile tea before she sleeps

Or tries to. Now she sighs, inhales the steam,
And swizzles Equal in to sweeten dream.

She finishes her drink and drifts to bed,
Her mind revolving all the daytime said.

The pillow might as well be of cement;
At last, near two a.m., her thoughts relent.

At seven-thirty—showered, oatmeal downed
And decaf pumped—she starts another round

And strides to bus stop, wearing perfect plan and hair:
Efficiency and friendliness. And prayer.

April Dusk

Dusk's apricot-almond sheath spreads
Behind blossomed branches' silhouette
And pine trees' hundred limbs of praise.
Pastel horizon yields to amber-reds
And marigold-maroon. Haze
And clarity join; pine limbs reach for jet.

Summer Dusk

Above horizon, phosphorescent moon
Flares evening silence over rose-maroon
Remaining haze from heat of noon.
Stars glint through opalescence, sparkle soon.

Car traffic thins but brightens, blaring lamps
Past evening silhouettes, down freeway ramps,
And into distant neighborhoods like camps
Recalling day's alliances, now strewn.

Commuter

Apartments like shelving line the block,
   Each unit up one number.
Commuters breakfast by the clock
   Beside stars' and streetlamps' penumbra.

The world arrives by data, wired,
   As engines warm and buses rumble.
Our marrow seethes—weary, wild!
   We dash, though, dawdle, ramble

To work, renew our effort with dawn—
   Time's orbit shedding yesterday.
Gulls swim champagne horizon.
   We gird for work; they seem to play.

A Meditation

Don't rush through leisure; bask
In clockless, warm, embracing bath.
Don't cram in respite; soak
In grassy shade beneath that oak,
And stroll not sprint through minutes. Breathe
Appreciation of the breeze.
Let moments pillow thought and slow
To pace at which the flowers grow.
Inhale massage. Recover reach
Of mind on now's eternal beach.
You know that worries, bills, and work await,
And you'll be punished if you're late.
So, stroll not sprint this weekend path,
Then soak in warm, embracing bath.

9 to 5 *

* On weekends he ignores the clock;
No deadline times his tasks. He strolls
Through errands; browses bookstores; bowls
And hikes; drinks in Baroque and rock

And jazz. He improvises, lets
His impulse wander: now, a snooze,
And later time to dine and schmooze
And ponder, exercise the legs

And mind, and sample leisure's menu. So,
Come Monday he commutes at dawn,
Reacclimates—despite a yawn—
To schedule and agenda, row

And list and column. Papers stack
On desk. He digs in, works. He's back.

Choice

I had a mediocre voice
And pregnant wife, raging rent
And some ambition, so my choice
Seemed clear: law school. And I went,

Got through, and lodged here at this firm
For thirty years, a "breadwinning Bob."
You well might ask: did I conform?
Perhaps. But take away my job,

Would I and family improve?
I cannot sing well. Of that there's proof.

Caravan

He leads his caravan of goals across
Fear's jungle, boredom's plain, and desert's loss.
A deluge drenches hope, and sunlight sears
And sweats resourcefulness that perseveres,
That knows to complement and balance. Health,
Love, friends, career, art, travel, social help—
His values jumpstart dawns to help him reach
His aims. If balanced, he can realize each.
Yet, here's no trail or shelter, and beyond—
A few oases. Treasure each safe pond.

Yet

You're tired, arms: I feel your ache and strain,
    Yet paychecks pull and lure,
Reward me. Lift, load, retrieve, retrain,
    And learn how to endure.

You're tired, legs: you stride all day, all week,
    Yet pride, care pull and lure,
Reward me. Hustle, hurry, whip, and wheel,
    And let the weekend cure.

You're tired, heart: you beat and pulse and jump
    Yet passions pull and lure,
Reward me. Peers admire how you pump
    Bloodwarmth through life impure.

You're tired, mind: you calculate, refine,
    Consider pull and lure.
You balance dream and skill, build nerve and spine,
    And learn, though still unsure.

Civilization

He preaches patience and restraint
Because indeed he's not a saint,
Would curse the kids and kick the couch,
Would scowl and rant like any grouch,
Would grudge a friend and spike her dream,
Raid lockers of her self-esteem.
No, he will pray and meditate,
Curb urge to spite, retaliate.
He yields, commits his heart to laws
Which clip the nails of lions' paws.

Love's Story

I'm made of low desire;
I'm made of noble aim.
I'm like a spreading fire;
I'm like a steady flame.

I'm made of stark obsession;
I'm made of calming plan.
I cherish indiscretion
Yet weigh taboo and ban.

I burst past bonds of reason;
I advocate restraint.
My bones feel like they're freezing
In fire, devil in a saint.

My seeming contradiction
Evolves each lustful day.
My love's complex, not fiction;
Dusk's scarlet, gold, and gray.

Microcosm

From this hilltop, that offstreet bar
Rollicking blue electric chords
For packed, inebriated hordes
Seems silversilent as a star
Or midnight lamp. Layperson grins
Trim courtesy and prim thought
Monday morning, having fought
For restraint that weekend against sins
He craves. Supernovae bomb
Where a mote tints night sky calm.

Suicide Notes

I

If I can't have her, we can't live
Alone. I lock her heart to my
Love, pulse, and passion. She can't leave
My blood. She warms cold secrets I
Can't reach. I've kissed her tantrums, blessed
Her ridicule, and joined her tears.
We're one in hand, in breath, at breast,
So now we'll join for all the years.

II

Restraining orders
Prove porous borders.
He'll kill for leaving
His crush. Start grieving.

Naïve young girl, withdraw from him
Who'd own your heart, who'd lock each limb
To his stare. Scoot, sprint, flee

When to keep your love he hides your key.

Freeway

The freeway lamps recede in lines
and curve into horizon haze,
beside them hillsides flecked with pines
and neighborhoods that nestle bays.

Hometown for most, where work and friends
and private dramas intersect.
Vacation spot for some, or fresh
start—here they'll struggle for success—

and for a few who drift on through
a place to hang around: what difference
what road or bed they choose, and who
cares. Comforted by distance

they leave as easily as they arrive.
Get on the freeway once again, and drive.

Flammable Material

—of a serial arsonist

For all his problems he will blame
Some others: his boss, some old flame
For whom he carries still his torch,
Some politicians—"all the same."
He'll teach them. He can singe—and scorch.
A match, a drop of fuel, a lighter
Can prove he's one effective fighter.

Balm

One inadvertent slight, a trifle,
Could yield a death from knife or rifle.
One glance of casual flirtation
Could spark a screaming confrontation.
One note of courteous rejection
Could stir a silent insurrection.
Yes, egos surge and seethe and blaze,
So posit in judicious phrase
The fault, well-mixed with tact and praise.

On Both Sides

My senses cue, inform, alert
    As sympathetic heart and mind
Imagine others' hurt
    And ways to salve. Now less confined

By what they sense around them, heart
    And mind approach ethereal
Admixture yielding art
    That yet respects material

Reality: a *Thank You* card,
    Bouquet of compliments, a gift
Certificate, accord
    Through dinner out, a game, a lift,

Free concert tickets, paid day off
    From job, a poem. Then, release
Of urge to heal. Enough
    Was offered—and, on both sides, peace.

Then

The gentlest jibe at his expense might sear
   His heart to dream revenge.
   One tactless slight might singe;
Soft elbow in the rib might seem a spear.

His pride would mutter threat and bullet spree,
   Would blaze volcanic cold
   That steamed and buried, killed
And only then might feel the slightest glee.

Yet, some co-workers taunted, pressed, and dared
   His heart to threaten, hate.
   They mocked his bulging weight,
Torn shirt, and sewn-up blue jeans. He endured

Until one afternoon. From cafeteria
   Police pulled seven corpses:
   Six co-workers and his.
A joke about his socks. Then, hysteria.

"A nice enough young man, although some odd
   Intensity could lurk."
   Wreaths, eulogies at work.
Bones holler grief behind routine's façade.

And Sunday—questions: why this spear from God?

Where

She hollers poetry at traffic, blames
The rooted hydrant for indifference;
Its water could not douse the flames
That lash her blood to scold existence.

She flails a bus with accusation
And squints her curses at a doorway, wall,
An alley. Then, brief contemplation
And mumbling slogging on while clutching all

Her stuff that fills a wrinkled garbage bag.
She totes her silence heavy now and weaves
Past stores. Where did her life begin to lag?
Her jacket cuffs are frayed but not the sleeves.

Margins

Despite night's scowl of wind and neon chill
And leering doorways, avenues,
And alleyways that know the kill,
Folks stroll about and shop, peruse.

They keep the *Space for Lease* signs off
These downtown shopfronts, feeding cash
To hungry registers. Enough
Folks buy, bless them, to fend off crash.

Ashcan Cathedral

Each dumpster hulks, backs butting brick façade,
This tar-patched puddled floor of canyon valley
Where van unloads delivery and truck
Discards the week's detritus. This alley
Seems stygian, a hiding place from God.
Yet even here, where drunken rotten luck
Might curse or kill or die
One still might glimpse the daytime sky.

Hearth in the Heart

The mother worries that her sons
Will join a gang and worship guns.
Her daughter, mother worries, could
Get raped in their own neighborhood.
As wife, she dreads her husband might
Get robbed and shot near work one night.

Her love attempts to shield them, bind
Their home into a haven for the kind.
Four willow branches reach from vase
On dining table gowned in lace.
A bowl of candies glitters near
The sofa Grandma left last year.

A cell phone, for emergencies,
Guards table, near where extra keys
Stay hidden. And just behind the vase
Lurk little canisters of mace.
From work, the mother telephones
Each afternoon. Firm, gentle tones

Remind the children of their chores
And mother's love—its keys, its doors.

QUESTIONS

Loosely based on newspaper reports, a call to a radio talk show, and a letter to an editor, these poems concern a fatal crash at dawn in Seattle between a police car and a bicycle ridden by a rock musician. The poems do not mean to precisely represent anyone involved in the event.

First Eyewitness

Man, that squad car's
Zooming, eighty, ninety, totals the bicycle,
And punts that guy's carcass to the stars.
Death slams into dawn, smears horizon red.
Fate's drunk, or that cop was. Guy was dead
Before he breathed again. He soared to Mars
And landed in his grave. Here I am still
Thinking morning's tarmac casket, shards and spars
Of bone and bike, that guy so vulnerable,
That light so red.

Police Officer

I didn't see the guy,
And now I'll always see him. Why
Take his life, Lord? I
Responded to emergency
And made a worse one. He
Flies in from nowhere. Suddenly
I dodge death and kill someone, green light
Turns morning scarlet. I answer a call
And cross and smash a man and wall.
We pay for error, huge or slight.

Mother

You whip through the intersection
Of life and chance and kill
With fellow police protection
And offer not a single note or call.
A sweeper clearing trash from gutter
Would by comparison seem warm.
Macadamize your heart, and putter
About that street in uniform:
A man—my glorious, musical son—
Hums silence to soil. Sorrow seeps
Through everything. The killing done,
Your cruiser drips oil; all else weeps.

Second Eyewitness

I told the inquest what I saw: the light was green.
The officer, he tried to slow
But that bike zoomed across his path
And flew to heaven. That's all I know.
You walk your dog at dawn—routine—
And watch some life become an aftermath.
You feel for the fella's family. And the cop:
He tried to be careful but couldn't stop.

Hard

In all that tangle and rubble
Of metal, body, glass, and rubber
Glints guilt. Actual facts
Survive all testimony and acts,
As do doubt and questions. Why,
Who, what, when—hard to know. Hard not to lie.

Realist

*—written after seeing a repairman
install a new water filter*

The filter, slicked in brownish goo,
Deleted from tap water rust,
Chlorine, lake algae, residue
From piping. If it snared lies too
That filter could restore some trust
To public life, to politics.
The conscience might then filter tricks,
Deceit—and yield words less untrue.

For Honesty

Honesty addresses and considers doubts
And questions—and can change.
It doesn't lock dissent in chains
Or answer evidence with threats and shouts.

Beguiling

The truth can mess and slop and mystify,
Embarrass, endanger, and ensnare—
But better true confusion or despair
Than a grinning, tidy lie.

On Incompetent Leadership

Incompetence cannot stay hidden
Though every protest be forbidden.
The apple's wax and cannot nourish,
The rose mere crêpe that cannot flourish,
The data virtual invention
Designed to neutralize dissension.
Folks know: they see the silver tarnish,
The wood still stained beneath the varnish.

HYPE AND HOPE

Golden Nation

A great and golden nation
Of prosperity and jobs!
A shakedown operation
Run by several dozen mobs.

Competitive Pricing

Covert authorities bug
Your flat? They want to know your drug—
Cars, clothes, food? Games, gadgets, porn? All yours
(Except privacy) shopping at their stores!

Building Community

You want to build community
And nurture culture's health?
Trust your own authenticity
And not some network's stealth.

Baited Hook

That person's soul is not your battlefield,
His life not advertising for your faith.
He knows what punishment dissent would yield
And that success means bribe when one must fake.
So, gadfly, responsible free spirit, stay
Sincere. Their promises mean you're their prey.

Unifier

You've honed religion to a science:
Manipulate and bribe,
Protected by your tribe,
And then buy others' silence.

Eenie-Meenie

The probing citizen votes but still hungers
For thoughtful candidates, not cliché-mongers.

For You to See

Betrayal might grin and call itself advice
And claim to cheer yet hope to undermine.
Recall: philosophers distinguish nice
From good. In life evil shows no underline.

Power

The hurricane, with whipping torque,
   Destroys the coastal village
But cannot sink a chip of cork
   Or make the people pillage.

Trustworthy

Amidst demagogic mud, he's firm
Footing; amidst disease, a germ
Of hope; amidst bribery, the pull
Of truth; in desert, an oasis pool.

Bird Person

I'd rather listen to a cockatoo screech
Than hear some noisy human preach.

Bounce

Grow resilient as the trampoline
Or be someone the world will trample on.

❉   ❉   ❉

Firefeathers

—for Sunny and Pickles

I forage like my forebears in the forest
On cage floor now, and in a chorus
Of two I shrill and shush and shriek
And preen my cohort's feathers and beak.
My owner, good woman, is not beguiled
By firefeathers; she knows I'm still half-wild.
Let avians buff my beak and her friends coo at bright
Orange and emerald coat. I can kiss, and bite.

Tropical Fish

Violet ripple afloat
In liquid silence, you shudder
Like a sail aflutter
On a tiny boat
As you drift aquarium seas
On kitchen countertop. You seldom cease
To undulate maroon, as watchers crave
Your world's fluid calm,
Your windowed water-home
For rippling fins of wave.

MISCHIEF AND MAJESTY

*—for Misha, Siamese
of Jan Nicosia and
Ian Schroeder*

Nest

From Misha's jeweled collar hang two metal pendants:
One gold, one blue—identifiers if she strays.
Unlikely, that. She might strut independence
But rarely roams. At home she dines and snoozes, plays
And strolls, is loved by owners—her attendants.

Classic

This Siamese will mew and purr,
Not yowl and bay and bawl
At noon, stars, window, wall.
A sole cloud isn't quieter.

Utility

Poor Misha can't remove her fur this hot
July noon, craves a cooler spot.
She mopes, ignores beloved toys, then naps
On bathroom floor, near laundry pile.
She wakes, stretches, yawns. Such sweet collapse
And luck! Fur softens tile!

Ecosystem

Now Misha sniffs her tuna, nibbles some,
Now nests in pillowed basket in the sun
And licks her paws and smooths her fur
And blesses house with mew and purr.

Now Misha's sleepy silence. Whiskers,
Brown tail and furry paws calm house to whispers.
Its harried humans read, hug, chat,
Steep tea, feel grateful for their cat.

Her Majesty

Now Grandma Annie's easy chair is Misha's throne.
Curved elm arms, cushioned carmine velveteen
With tufted back can serve this feline queen
Whose tail and paws stand guard: *the chair's for me alone.*

❋ ❋ ❋

Blade

Knife's serried blade can slice the juicy roast
And smother marmalade across hot toast.
Its steel can carve a chicken to a meal,
Can mangle human flesh or pare to heal.
Utensil, tool, or weapon, knife could kill,
Stays loyal subject to some human will.
Now done preparing lunch, his kitchen kempt,
The cook stores knife in drawer, will not tempt
The temper. Now, the woodsman stores his knife
In leather sheath, protecting blade—and life.

Spoonful

This little scoop, this steel cupped hand, lifts soup
To hungry mouth, stirs spice in broth, and blends
The honey in the tea. It measures soap
And oil, medicine and meal, extends
The reach of arm and hand. This spoon might whirl
Ingredients to make them one, but we
Can stop the stir, can note refraction's pearl
In glass of water, sip its imagery.

Boxful

You could store so much in a cardboard box—
Old clothes; new linen; not-quite-favorite books;
A fan in autumn; blankets in July;
Small garden tools; rough drafts, and each reply
From lover; catcher's mitt and mask and pads;
Diplomas, diaries, and residue from fads;
Unwanted gifts; snapshots, souvenirs, and stuff
We cannot quite discard, that somehow's tough
To purge—distinctive, oddly poignant, or
Perhaps of use still. So we keep, we store
And treasure in a box or memory.
That concert program. Her sonnet. To me.

GRAB BAG

It's Raining!

Umbrellas bloom beneath the drizzle,
And traffic's zoom begins to sizzle.

A Climatological Observation

Some complain about Seattle's rain
Simply because they like to complain.

Grape

Taut jade oval, you splash tart
Juice on tongue and sweeten heart.
Healthy liquor bathing blood
Once was raindrop prinking mud.

On Listening to Popular Songs

These songs a waste of time? They lubricate
My bones and tendons, syncopate
Vitality through mind, make instinct snap
Its fingers, grin, and start to clap!

Carpe Diem

Try to empty your basket
Before you fill your casket.

Railings

Those long metal railings
Beside the freeway
Help mitigate failings
And give us leeway.

Builder

Though burdens overwhelm and crush,
Do not escape from them—or rush
To finish. Be a patient builder:
Lift pebbles when you cannot budge a boulder.

Notebook

Yes, in your notebook scratch some doggerel!
So what? You need to stretch, not let it
Worry ego every phrase is not immortal.
Moreover, when you publish, you can edit.

Improvement

You resolve to improve but fail
To reach your goal. Relax, you're doing fine!
You needn't castigate and rail.
You'll get there, though not in a perfect line.

Through Integrity

Now, budget forecasts fall. Your enterprise could end
As patron, customer, and friend
Dread losses. Don't, though, imitate some trend
To lure them in. Though autumn leaves might disappear
They're popular each year.

Continuum

He bends fate, squeezes from his worst mistake
His greatest lucky break.

Balanced

Love and laughter link body and brain:
Reason alone can't keep us sane.

Young

Tender shoots
Need sturdy roots.

Note to a Boy

You almost bumped that woman! Growing
Means learning to look where you're going.

Data

Those who feel like a statistic
Can often become sadistic.

Independent

"We love indie films, theaters, record labels, indie … "
Or perhaps you love the hip, the cool, the trendy.

Not Simply

Poetry: not made of statistics
But not simply for mystics.

Push and Pause

Day's data and deadlines,
Dusk's bus crowds and headlines.

Night's lamp and book, tea or wine,
Heart's pause on a timeless line.

Note on Rhyme

Affection for rhyme might be innate,
Reflecting wish to connect and mate.

Literary Fame

Fame might be superficial, fleeting,
But it attracts folks to your reading.

Rhymes

Yes, rhyming *moon* and *June* is obvious
But *moon* and *rune* or *moon* and *strewn* are less
So. Rhyming can be subtle: *moon* and *croon,*
Festoon. Rhymes needn't be clichéd or crude.

To a Demanding Critic

You now expect a masterpiece
Each time I lift a pen.
You think I whip off classics when I please?
You write such pieces, then!

Tribes

Magistrates
Love memoranda.
Dogmatists
Love propaganda.
Artists love
None of the above.

Gift

A gift does not bribe. It will not stick
To your hands nor make you sick
With guilt. You might dislike it, yet
It never calls itself your debt.

Leadership Fund

One million bucks per year—his living—
To preach and cheerlead selfless giving.

To Some Sports Fans

Get on the field yourself and scrum
Before you call that player *Bum!*

To a Stressed Athlete

Seek victory? Like seeking happiness or praise:
Directly rarely works. Just make your plays.

Rebounder

His knees and elbows—hinges and joints:
He bends them sharply, makes his points.

Blood on Sand

Tales of gladiators prove "the glory
That was Rome" was awfully gory.

Plenty as It Is

Create a "hell"? God didn't need to bother.
He simply left us with each other.

Goodness

"Ah," Good Intention cries, "we now can fix up
The situation!"—or deepen the mix-up.

Mask

Ideologue spouts an –ism
To mask a self that isn't.

Creativity, 3:00 a.m.

Lust can erupt at inconvenient times,
Like rage or hunger, tears or thirst, or rhymes.

St. Valentine's Day

The heart-shaped chocolate box, the dozen roses,
The pinkmist card to *My Sweet Valentine*
With golden necklace and red bottled wine
Could kindle love, could mask mere poses.

Libido

Libido: locomotive loose
In my own blood—my brain's the caboose!

Kin

The body—lust converses with restraint.
A savage dwells beside a saint.

Core Values

Reminder: lust can crave and rage and roar
And stands with reason at our core.

Pornography

Doff it
For profit.

Of a Friend's Modeling

A bare body can fill
A bare cupboard or till.

True Love

Demark true love from lust and sex?
They often intersect.

Of the Temptation

Lust tests restraint and tempts fidelity,
Which sighs and hums romantic melody.

Lust's Lesson

Each heart contains a point like a button
That, pressed, can change restraint to a glutton.

Nocturnal Noon

Lean silence, with sharp claws for fight:
At noon the feline prowls the night.

Separate Ways

No need for fear or grief.
Without offense I took your hints.
Decision yields relief.
Now shower me away, and rinse.

For Hatha Yoga

These twists and stretches squeeze
The hurry from my heart
And loosen knots of stress
Between my shoulders. Bless
These simple postures, art
Of patience, limber ease.

Value

He won't waste money, but he pampers
His health. At sixty, he still scampers!

Dancers

With lilt and leap in legs and feet they wheel
About the pub to jig and reel!

Love's End: Natural Course

I feel more relieved than sad or hollow.
Leaves fall, streams freeze. Springtime, though, will follow.

Not One Nor Two

Regrets about our love? Not one—
Neither the love, nor that it's done.

Hmm …

She filters him throughout her soul,
Open to loving him whole,
But if she once suspects he lies,
She'll close the gate behind her eyes.

Absolutely

"This will be my final decision!"
Typically precedes yet more revision.

Next?

What first seems cursed might yield a blessing.
Life's complex—and keeps us guessing.

❋   ❋   ❋

Other Galaxies

Admire twilight's salmon-ruby mist,
Stars' silver scatter, turquoise-gray dawn;
Recall at noon other galaxies exist
As human pettiness smirks and smatters
And self-importance boasts and chatters.
Let them. Persist with *your* work, until it's done.

In Seeming Silence

Evergreen hillside

     serries

          horizon. Crossing the bay a ferry's

               lamps glide.

Last Issue

—for Troxey Kemper (1915–2002),
Tucumcari Literary Review *editor*

You published dozens of my epigrams
And quatrains, quirky rhyming bits.
Now, you, the master quilter who crammed
So much rhymed verse into each issue, fit
Inside a simple coffin. May this
Sestet show we remember and miss.

Ridge and Roofline

As day awakens, streetlamps drowse, almost yawn.
The evergreen ridge, and rooflines, and gulls
Above the bridge appear; the freeway chants wan
Concrete shadow beneath translucent moon and lulls
The neighborhoods. The bay breathes
Silver sky beneath magenta sheaths
Of cloud. Now the streetlamps doze.
A bus zooms somewhere, and light
Infuses city with gray detail and rose
Renewal, still whispering the night.

Within Horizon

Gulls' silhouettes recede through waves
Of saffron feather cirrus. Streetlamps gleam
Along the bridge, from bluff to hill,
And colonize the neighborhoods with dream.

The gulls flap distance over bridge, then leave
Past bridge's steady traffic flow
To land upon invisibility
Within horizon's salmon glow.

Yet more gulls hover over harbor, as chill
Prompts evening shiver. Gulls scud, weave
Through amber-ruby, swoop possibility
Through darkness, scamper till the dawn awakes.

David D. Horowitz founded and manages Rose Alley Press. He earned bachelor's degrees in philosophy and English from the University of Washington and a master's degree in English from Vanderbilt University. His most recent poetry collections, published by Rose Alley Press, are *Streetlamp, Treetop, Star* and *Resin from the Rain*. Many of his poems are first published in fine literary journals, and he gives frequent readings. David lives and works in Seattle.

Photograph by Ed Goralnick

Other *Rose Alley Press Titles*

Caruso for the Children, & Other Poems by William Dunlop, 0-9651210-2-X, paper, $9.95
"Dunlop is a brilliant metrical technician.... richly allusive, a gifted parodist, and often very funny."
—Jonathan Raban

Rain Psalm, poems by Victoria Ford, 0-9651210-0-3, paper, $5.95
"Victoria Ford's poems are at once modest and courageous, cut clean and sure ... " —Sam Hamill

From Notebook to Bookshelf: Four Pamphlets About Writing, Publishing, & Marketing
by David D. Horowitz, 0-9745024-1-3, coil, $4.95

Resin from the Rain, poems by David D. Horowitz, 0-9651210-8-9, paper, $9.95
"The office worker's plight, the murder in the papers, the lonely streetwalker at dusk all find residence in Horowitz's humanity." —Derek Sheffield

Streetlamp, Treetop, Star, poems by David D. Horowitz, 0-9651210-5-4, paper, $9.95
" ... an excellent new book—authentic 'words ... to cleanse even the sharpest wounds.'"
—Carol Robertshaw

Strength & Sympathy: Essays & Epigrams by David D. Horowitz, 0-9651210-1-1, paper, $8.95
" ... incisive essays and epigrams that take us from proper pronouns to considerate theology."
—Míceál F. Vaughan

On Paper Wings, poems by Donald Kentop, 0-9745024-0-5, paper, $6.95
"Donald Kentop writes with an assurance that invites the reader into his poems.... This is an accomplished and memorable collection." —Richard Wakefield

To Enter the Stillness, poems by Douglas Schuder, 0-9651210-7-0, paper, $6.95
"Douglas Schuder brings uncommonly graceful phrasing to everything he sees."
—David Mason

Adam Chooses, poems by Michael Spence, 0-9651210-4-6, paper, $9.95
" ... the elegant design and the formal ease we've come to expect of Michael Spence's work."
—Madeline DeFrees

Weathered Steps, poems by Joannie Kervran Stangeland, 0-9651210-9-7, paper, $6.95
"*Weathered Steps* is a book about all that you almost don't notice, but should."
—Melinda Mueller

Rose Alley Press
David D. Horowitz, President
4203 Brooklyn Avenue NE, #103A
Seattle, WA 98105-5911
Telephone: 206-633-2725
E-mail: rosealleypress@juno.com
Web site: www.rosealleypress.com